LOOKING AT COUNTRIES

Looking at
VENEZUELA

Kathleen Pohl

Reading consultant: Susan Nations, M.Ed.,
author/literacy coach/consultant in literacy development

Gareth Stevens
Publishing

Please visit our web site at www.garethstevens.com.
For a free color catalog describing Gareth Stevens Publishing's list
of high-quality books, call 1-800-542-2595 (USA) or 1-800-387-3178 (Canada).
Gareth Stevens Publishing's fax: 1-877-542-2596

Library of Congress Cataloging-in-Publication Data

Pohl, Kathleen.
        Looking at Venezuela / Kathleen Pohl.
                p. cm. — (Looking at countries)
        Includes bibliographical references and index.
        ISBN-10: 0-8368-9074-4   ISBN-13: 978-0-8368-9074-7 (lib.bdg.)
        ISBN-10: 0-8368-9075-2   ISBN-13: 978-0-8368-9075-4 (softcover)
        1. Venezuela—Juvenile literature. I. Title.
F2308.5.P64   2009
987—dc22   2008003107

This edition first published in 2009 by
Gareth Stevens Publishing
A Weekly Reader® Company
1 Reader's Digest Road
Pleasantville, NY 10570-7000 USA

Senior Managing Editor: Lisa M. Herrington
Senior Editor: Barbara Bakowski
Creative Director: Lisa Donovan
Designer: Tammy West
Photo Researcher: Charlene Pinckney

Photo credits: (t=top, b=bottom, l=left, r=right, c=center)
Cover © James Sparshatt/Corbis; title page Will & Deni McIntyre/Getty Images;
p. 4 Pablo Corral V/Corbis; p. 6 James Marshall/Corbis; p. 7t Ed Darack; p. 7b
Theo Allofs/Getty Images; p. 8 Shutterstock (2); p. 9 Superstock; p. 10 Nicholas Pitt/Alamy;
p. 11t Paula Bronstein/Getty Images; p. 11b Krzysztof Dydynski/Lonely Planet Images;
p. 12 John R. Kreul/Independent Picture Service/CFWimages.com; p. 13 Pablo Corral V/
Corbis; p. 14 Kevin Schafer/Corbis; p. 15t Pablo Corral V/Corbis; p. 15b Robert Caputo/
Aurora/Getty Images; p. 16 Hisham F. Ibrahim/Getty Images; p. 17t Juan Silva/The Image Bank/
Getty Images; p. 17b David Frazier/Corbis; p. 18 Shutterstock (2); p. 19t Pablo Corral V/Corbis;
p. 19b Robert Caputo/Aurora/Getty Images; p. 20t Rita Maas/Jupiter; p. 20b Sean Sprague/Alamy;
p. 21 Marion Kaplan/Alamy; p. 22l Leslie Mazoch/AP; p. 22r Steve Starr/Corbis; p. 23 Juan Silva/
Getty Images; p. 24 Jim McIsaac/Getty Images; p. 25t Ken Welsh/Alamy; p. 25b Krzysztof Dydynski/
LPI/Getty Images; p. 26 Shutterstock; p. 27t, c David Rochkind/Bloomberg News/Landov;
p. 27b Art Wolfe/Getty Images

Printed in the United States of America

1 2 3 4 5 6 7 8 9 11 10 09 08

Contents

Words that appear in the glossary are printed in **boldface** type the first time they occur in the text.

Where Is Venezuela?

Venezuela lies at the northern tip of the **continent** of South America. It shares borders with three countries. Guyana is to the east, and Brazil is to the south. To the west is Colombia. To the north, Venezuela has a long coast on the Caribbean Sea. Many small islands off the coast are part of Venezuela.

Did you know?

Venezuela is one of the top 10 oil-producing countries in the world.

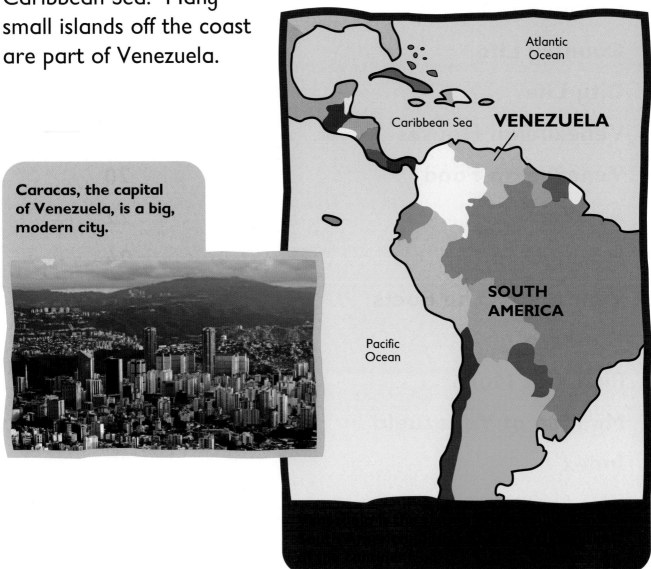

Caracas, the capital of Venezuela, is a big, modern city.

Atlantic Ocean

Caribbean Sea

VENEZUELA

SOUTH AMERICA

Pacific Ocean

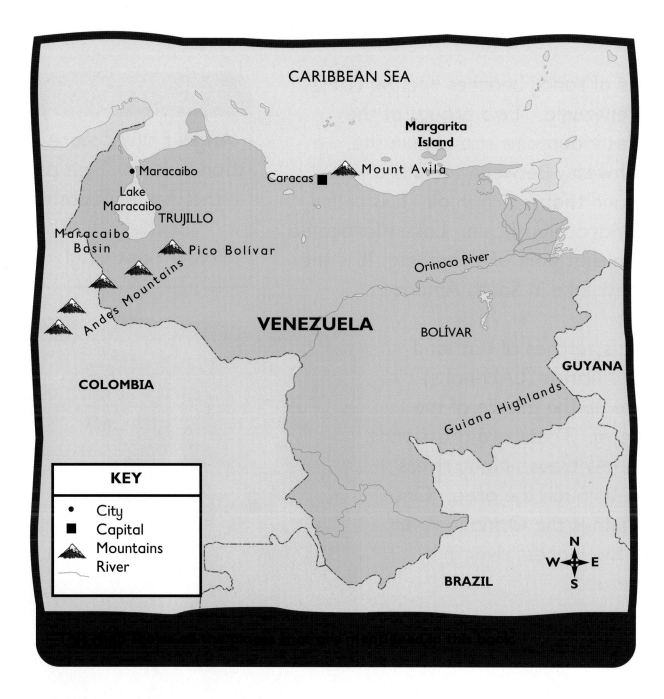

Venezuela is about twice the size of the state of California. Caracas is the capital and the biggest city. It is the center of government. Caracas is a rich and modern city, but many poor people live there, too.

The Landscape

Miles of sandy beaches line the coast of Venezuela. Two groups of the Andes Mountains rise high in the northwest. Between them is a lowland that is rich in oil. It is called the Maracaibo Basin. Lake Maracaibo lies in that part of Venezuela. It is the biggest lake in South America.

Long stretches of flat land called **llanos** (LAH-nohs) make up the middle of the country. These are grasslands with few trees. Many rivers flow through the area. One of them is the Orinoco River. It is the longest river in Venezuela.

Did you know?

Angel Falls is more than twice as high as the Empire State Building in New York City!

Angel Falls is the highest waterfall in the world! Many people come from other countries to see the falls.

Flat-topped stone cliffs, called tepui, rise in the Guiana Highlands.

The **capybara** is the largest rodent in the world. It looks like a big guinea pig. The capybara lives near swamps and lakes.

The Guiana Highlands, in the southeast, have many **tepui** (tay-PWEE). Those are stone cliffs with flat tops. This region is home to Angel Falls. It is the highest waterfall in the world! Thick **rain forests** cover the south. Many rare kinds of plants and animals live there.

Weather and Seasons

Venezuela has a **tropical** climate. It is hot in the low regions. The mountain areas are cooler. Snow covers some peaks in the Andes year round. The weather in Caracas is pleasantly warm. The city sits in a valley in the mountains near the sea. A valley is an area of lowland between mountain ranges.

Caracas lies at the foot of Mount Avila. Heavy rains sometimes cause mudslides on the mountain slopes.

There are two seasons, a wet and a dry season. The dry season lasts from November through May. The wet season goes from June through October. Rain falls mostly in the mountains and in the thick forests of the south. On the coast, the climate is mostly dry.

Did you know?

Pico Bolívar is the highest peak in Venezuela. It is one of the few places where snow falls.

The dry season on the llanos lasts for many months. During the wet season, the rivers there sometimes flood.

Venezuelan People

Twenty-four million people live in Venezuela. The oil business has made some of them very rich. Many others belong to the middle class. They have good jobs, take vacations, and live and dress well. One of every three people, however, is poor.

The Caribs (KA-rubz) and the Arawaks (A-ruh-wahks) were the first people in Venezuela.

Did you know?

Many Venezuelan parents like to give their children unusual names. Sometimes parents name their children after famous people. Sometimes they combine two names or use an uncommon spelling.

A woman holds a rosary as she prays. She is Roman Catholic, like most people in Venezuela.

Girls in colorful folk costumes dance at a festival.

Later, Spain ruled the country for 300 years. The Spanish brought black slaves with them. Today, most people in Venezuela have a mixed background.

Spanish is the main language. Some people speak English, too. In far-off villages, some groups still speak their native language.

Most people in Venezuela follow the Roman Catholic religion. A few are Protestant. There are very small numbers of Jews and Muslims.

School and Family

Children between the ages of six and 15 must go to school. Many younger children attend preschool. Free public school is available to all. In the countryside, some children go to one-room schools.

In primary school, children learn reading, writing, and math. They learn history and science, too.

Did you know?

Rich and poor families in Venezuela often have eight or nine children. Middle-class families are smaller, with two or three children.

This family enjoys an outing in a city park. Most families in Venezuela are large.

When they are older, some students go to trade schools to learn job skills. Other students go on to college. Nine out of 10 Venezuelans ages 15 and older can read and write.

Most families in Venezuela are large. Children, parents, and grandparents might all live in the same home. Family is an important part of daily life in Venezuela. Relatives visit often to celebrate weddings, birthdays, and holidays.

Country Life

One out of every 10 people lives in the country. Many of them own or **rent** small farms. They grow just enough food for their families. Crops usually include beans, corn, and rice. On very big farms called **plantations**, workers grow coffee, cocoa, sugarcane, and fruits to be sold.

On the flat llanos, cowboys tend big herds of cattle. They work for ranch owners who raise beef and dairy cattle. On the coast, some people fish for tuna, crabs, clams, and shrimp.

The coffee beans on these trees are almost ripe. Workers pick the coffee beans by hand.

Many people who live in the country or in small towns are poor. Some do not have running water or power for lights. The government runs programs to help poor people improve their lives.

City Life

Over the past 60 years, many people have moved to the cities to work. Today, most people in Venezuela live in cities. Most of the cities are in the north, near the sea. They are very crowded. The streets are filled with cars and buses.

Did you know?

Like most Spanish cities, Caracas has a main square, or plaza, at its center.

Pretty clothing at a street market catches this shopper's eye.

Many people ride the subway in Caracas. The trains travel underground.

More than 4 million people live in and around Caracas. Many of them are poor. They live in shacks, called **ranchos**, on the edge of the city. This modern capital has new houses, tall office buildings, and a busy airport, too. Restaurants, shops, and museums line some of the streets.

Maracaibo is Venezuela's second-biggest city. Only Caracas is home to more people. Maracaibo is also a key port. Products such as coffee, leather, and chocolate are shipped from there to other countries. Most of Maracaibo's wealth, however, comes from the oil fields nearby.

Venezuelan Houses

In the cities, many middle-class people live in high-rise apartment buildings. Some apartments have a balcony, or an upper porch.

Many rich people own big houses with pretty gardens. The rooms are built around a courtyard. The houses have tile roofs and brightly colored walls.

There is a shortage of housing for people in Venezuela. More than I million new homes are needed in the overcrowded cities. The government has promised to build low-cost houses.

This Spanish-style house has a tile roof.

Ranchos crowd the hills outside Caracas. Poor people build their tiny homes from scraps of wood.

In settlements on the edge of the cities, poor people live in one-room ranchos. Ranchos have mud walls and dirt floors. Many of the huts are built of wood scraps. The roofs are usually made of **thatched** palm leaves.

On the coast and along the Orinoco River, many houses sit on stilts. The tall wooden poles keep the homes above the water.

Many people who live along the Orinoco River build their houses on stilts. The tall poles keep the water's edge above the water.

Did you know?

The name *Venezuela* means "little Venice." When Spanish explorers first saw stilt houses there, they thought of Venice, Italy. Venice is a city built over water.

Venezuelan Food

People in Venezuela typically eat a lot of beans and rice. They like **arepas** (ah-RAY-pahs), too. Arepas are soft cornmeal cakes filled with eggs, meat, or cheese. Most Venezuelans also eat beef, chicken, fish, and fresh fruits. They drink plenty of coffee. Coffee is one of the country's main crops.

Arepas look like small pancakes made of cornmeal. They can be filled with meat or cheese to make a kind of sandwich.

Ripe coffee beans are called "cherries" because they turn red.

Men at a market sell fresh fish from the Orinoco River. Fish is often served with rice and stews.

Lunch is the biggest meal of the day. It often includes soup, salad, meat, vegetables, and dessert. After lunch, many people take a **siesta**, or nap. Then they go back to work or school. People usually eat a light dinner late at night.

Venezuelans shop for food at grocery stores and outdoor markets. Different parts of the country are known for different foods. For example, Trujillo (troo-HEE-yoh) is famous for its pastries. Bolívar is known for tasty fish stews.

> **Did you know?**
>
> **Hallacas**
> (ah-YAH-cas) are special Christmas treats in Venezuela. They are cornmeal pies stuffed with beef, pork, chicken, and spices. The pies are wrapped in leaves and then boiled.

At Work

Oil is Venezuela's most important **natural resource**. A natural resource is something supplied by nature that people use for industry. Oil is Venezuela's biggest **export**, or product sold to other countries. Many people work in the oil fields.

Did you know?

The United States buys much of Venezuela's oil to run homes, businesses, and cars.

At **refineries**, such as the one shown here, oil is made into gasoline and other products.

Some farmers use modern equipment to harvest rice. Rice is one of Venezuela's most important food crops.

Some people work in mining. Venezuela is rich in coal, iron ore, and gold. One-tenth of the country's workers are farmers. Others fish for a living. A few work in the **timber** industry.

Some people have service jobs. They work in stores, banks, offices, and museums. Others are doctors, nurses, or teachers. Many people who have jobs in **tourism** work in hotels and restaurants. They may also be tour guides or work in national parks.

Having Fun

People in Venezuela enjoy sports, especially baseball and soccer. They play sports on the streets and at school. They watch professional teams play at large stadiums. In some cities, bullfighting is popular. Many people also like to play tennis or hike in the mountains.

Venezuelans and tourists enjoy rafting on the Orinoco River. The country's many lakes are good places for swimming, water-skiing, and fishing. Many people also go horseback riding in the Andes or on the llanos.

Did you know?

Most towns in Venezuela hold a fiesta, or party, each year to honor their **patron saint**. People say that the saint watches over the village.

Tourists enjoy paddling a dugout canoe in one of Venezuela's national parks.

Folk musicians entertain listeners in a village in the Andes Mountains.

Young people enjoy dancing at nightclubs. **Salsa** is a popular fast dance with plenty of rhythm! At folk festivals, musicians play a four-string guitar called a **cuatro**. They shake **maracas**, which are rattles made from dried gourds.

Carnival is a major holiday in Venezuela. During this four-day festival, many businesses are closed. People celebrate with dance, music, balloons, and parades.

Venezuela: The Facts

• Venezuela is a federal **republic**. The national government and the states have separate powers. Elected officials represent the people.

• Citizens who are 18 or older may vote.

• The people of Venezuela elect the president, who serves for six years. The president can serve a second term. The president is the head of the national government.

• Spain ruled Venezuela for 300 years. Venezuela gained its independence, or freedom, in 1811.

The flag of Venezuela has three bars. The top bar is yellow. The blue bar in the middle has eight white stars. The bottom bar is red.

- The official name of Venezuela is República Bolivariana de Venezuela (Bolivarian Republic of Venezuela). Símon Bolívar was one of the leaders in Venezuela's fight for freedom.

- Spanish is the official language of Venezuela.

Left: Venezuela's unit of money is the **bolívar fuerte**, or "strong bolivar." Inset: The 12½-cent coin is in use again.

A tiny frog peers out from an orchid. The frog and the flower live in the hot, wet rain forest.

Glossary

arepas — soft cornmeal cakes that are wrapped around fillings such as meat or fruit

bolívar fuerte — Venezuela's unit of money

capybara — a large rodent that can grow to be 4 feet long

continent — one of the main landmasses of Earth

cuatro — a Venezuelan guitar with four strings

export — a product sold and sent to another country

hallacas — cornmeal pies that are stuffed with meat and spices, wrapped in leaves, and boiled

llanos — vast grassy plains in the middle of Venezuela

maracas — dried gourds with seeds inside that rattle when they are shaken

natural resource — things supplied by nature, such as forests and minerals, that are used by people

patron saint — a saint who is thought to protect a person or a place

plantations — huge farms where hired workers grow and harvest a single crop

rain forests — very thick forests in tropical climates where tall trees form a canopy over other trees and plants

ranchos — one-room shacks built from scraps by poor people in Venezuela

refineries — areas of towers, pipes, and pumps where oil is made into gasoline and other products

rent — to pay money to the owner for the use of a house or an apartment

republic — a kind of government in which decisions are made by the people of the country and their representatives

salsa — a fast, rhythmic dance that is popular in many Latin American countries

siesta — the Spanish word for "nap"

tepui — flat-topped mountains in the Guiana Highlands

thatched — made of bundles of grass, palm leaves, or straw

timber — trees and their wood, which is used in building

tourism — the business of serving tourists, or people who travel for pleasure

tropical — having a hot and humid climate

Find Out More

Embassy of Venezuela in the United States
www.embavenez-us.org

Fact Monster: Venezuela
www.factmonster.com/ipka/AO108140.html

Travel the World with A to Z Kids Stuff
www.atozkidstuff.com/ven.html

Zoom Rainforests
www.zoomschool.com/subjects/rainforest

Publisher's note to educators and parents: Our editors have carefully reviewed these Web sites to ensure that they are suitable for children. Many Web sites change frequently, however, and we cannot guarantee that a site's future contents will continue to meet our high standards of quality and educational value. Be advised that children should be closely supervised whenever they access the Internet.

My Map of Venezuela

Photocopy or trace the map on page 31. Then write in the names of the countries, bodies of water, cities, land areas, and states listed below. (Look at the map on page 5 if you need help.)

After you have written in the names of all the places, find some crayons and color the map!

Countries
Brazil
Colombia
Guyana
Venezuela

Bodies of Water
Caribbean Sea
Lake Maracaibo
Orinoco River

Cities
Caracas
Maracaibo

Land Areas and Mountains
Andes Mountains
Guiana Highlands
Maracaibo Basin
Margarita Island
Pico Bolívar

States
Bolívar
Trujillo

Index